Kangaroos

Kangaroos

ON LOCATION

KATHY DARLING

PHOTOGRAPHS BY TARA DARLING

LOTHROP, LEE & SHEPARD BOOKS   NEW YORK

ACKNOWLEDGMENTS

Dr. John Kirsch, Director of the University of Wisconsin Zoological Museum. Thank you for sharing your firsthand knowledge of kangaroos and for checking the manuscript for accuracy.

Dr. Richard Taylor of Harvard University whose knowledge of kangaroo movement was generously shared.

Lindsay Smith of the Australian Overseas Information Service and the Tasmanian Tourist Board, the Queensland Tourist Board, the South Australian Tourist Board, and the Western Australia Tourist Board for helping us find research sites.

The Bloxham Family of Planet Downs Ranch, for showing us how deeply committed some Australians are to preserving the natural world.

Cradle Mountain Lodge, Tasmania. A haven for little kangaroos. Special thanks to Cary Scotton.

O'Reilly's Guest House, Green Mountains, Queensland. A magical place surrounded by birds and flowers, and hopping with kangaroos and a staff that cares.

Text copyright © 1993 by Mary Kathleen Darling
Photographs copyright © 1993 by Tara Darling

Library of Congress Cataloging in Publication   Darling, Kathy.   Kangaroos on location / Kathy Darling : photographs by Tara Darling.   p.   cm.   Includes index.   Summary: Discusses the physical characteristics and behavior of different varieties of kangaroos.   ISBN 0-688-09728-6.—ISBN 0-688-09729-4 (lib. bdg.)   1. Kangaroos—Juvenile literature. [1. Kangaroos.]   I. Darling, Tara, ill.   II. Title.   QL737.M35D36   1993   599.2—dc20   92-38418   CIP   AC

Contents

The Wonder Down Under

Australia's first European explorers saw strange animals, as tall as a man, leaping like giant grasshoppers. They could hardly believe their eyes. It is said that they asked the natives the name of the unknown animals and the aborigines replied, "Kangaroo." It meant "I don't understand you," but the Europeans thought it referred to the strange hopping creatures and named them kangaroos.

The kangaroo is not a single species; it is a family of animals—a big family. There are sixty different kinds of kangaroos and twelve close relatives called rat kangaroos. They were a wonder to European explorers because they are native only to Australia and nearby islands.

Although they are all related, the kangaroos range in size from 2 to 200 pounds. Their social organizations vary, too. The small forest-dwelling species are most often solitary; medium-sized 'roos live in families; and the large grassland nomads travel in groups called mobs. The most common colors are blue, gray, and red, but kangaroos can also be black, yellow, or brown. Sometimes their soft fur is patterned with stripes or rings. There are many names for the different kinds of kangaroos: wallaby, wallaroo, pademelon, euro, and forester. But there are no *important* differences in either body or brain among the 100 million members of the family.

Bennett's wallaby joeys

7

Australia, sometimes called the Land Down Under, has many kinds of environments. Most of the variations in kangaroos are adaptations to the different habitats. Our search for wild kangaroos took us across thousands of miles. We saw kangaroos bounding across the open plains, just as we expected. But we were as surprised as the early explorers when we found kangaroos climbing in trees, running through snow tunnels, swimming in lakes, and leaping off cliffs in the dark.

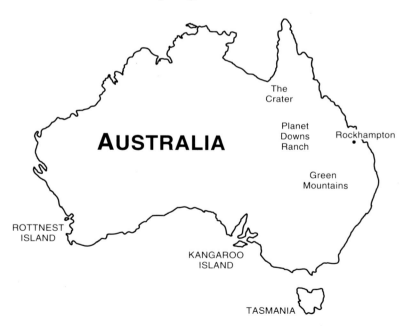

AUSTRALIA

The Crater

Planet Downs Ranch

Rockhampton

Green Mountains

ROTTNEST ISLAND

KANGAROO ISLAND

TASMANIA

THE CRATER *Lumholtz tree kangaroos* live in The Crater National Park, but they are hard to find. That's because they spend 99 percent of their time sleeping or munching leaves high in the rain-forest canopy.

We expected tree kangaroos to be great jumpers, leaping gracefully from limb to limb. The truth is, they are rather clumsy and accidents are common. Moving from one tree to another is a cautious affair involving all four feet. Tree kangaroos seem to be very good at crash landings, often surviving a 50- or 60-foot fall without serious injury. On the ground, tree kangaroos hop like other kangaroos.

Both the *red-necked* and *red-legged pademelon* are found in the undergrowth of the rain forest.

◀ *The search for kangaroos took us to these places in Australia.*

The fur on a Lumholtz tree kangaroo's shoulders is parted so that water is directed away from the face—a handy hairdo to have in the rain forest. ▶

TASMANIA This mountainous island off the southeast coast is cold, even in the summer. In the winter the shaggy-furred *Bennett's wallabies* dig tunnels in the snow. Although they are nocturnal like other kangaroos, Bennetts sometimes feed in daylight if the weather is chilly enough.

In the high country, where snowfall is heavy, *Tasmanian pademelons* use their forepaws to uncover buried vegetation. Pademelons are especially shy. We never saw one in the daytime. Even at night they rarely venture more than one hundred yards from the safety of forest thickets.

PLANET DOWNS RANCH   *Eastern grey kangaroos* share the grassland with cattle on this huge ranch owned by the Bloxham family. Planet Downs is typical of the habitat preferred by greys: mixed grassland and forest.

Greys and reds, the largest of the kangaroos, grow throughout their lives. Some of the ranch's "boomers," as the males are called, are 7 feet tall on their tiptoes and weigh 200 pounds. The females, known as "fliers," are less than half that size and are so different in appearance that they are often mistaken for a separate species.

The Bloxhams take pride in the abundant native wildlife found on their cattle ranch and provide them with sanctuary, food, and water.

◀ *Tasmanian pademelons are extinct on mainland Australia, but these small forest kangaroos are still common in Tasmania's cool rain forests.*

A kangaroo's *foot is more than a foot long. Species with feet shorter than 12 inches are called* wallabies *or* pademelons. *The eastern grey buck has 18-inch hind feet.* ▶

11

ROCKHAMPTON *Rock wallabies* are the acrobats of the kangaroo world. Their cliff dancing, daredevil leaps, and balancing acts on narrow ledges must be seen to be believed. When they are disturbed, mobs bound up preplanned escape routes with lightning speed. Knobby skin on their feet grips the rocks like a tire grips the road. Extra-thick padding cushions their landings, and very flexible toes help them hang on. Even with these aids, a mother rock wallaby has trouble leaping around with a big baby in her pouch. So, unlike the other kangaroos, rock wallaby mothers leave half-grown joeys in caves and other hiding places when they go down from the cliffs at night to eat.

Most rock wallabies are noted for their beautiful fur color and markings. The ones we watched at Rockhampton are plain—so plain that they are called the *unadorned rock wallaby.*

◄ *The unadorned rock wallaby uses its long tail to balance when it hops up and down cliffs.*

As you might expect from an animal nicknamed "stinker," swamp wallabies live alone.

GREEN MOUNTAINS *Swamp wallabies* are little hunchbacked kangaroos. They hop bent over in order to get through the thick undergrowth of their tropical rainforest home. Maintaining a network of tunnels that are just big enough to squeeze through, the swamp wallabies race along them at full speed with head low and tail stuck straight out. Imagine how tough these wallabies are. It's not every kangaroo that can live in swamps or eat orchids, ferns, or plants that are poisonous to almost all other animals.

ROTTNEST ISLAND *Quokkas,* one of our favorite kangaroos, live here. The name of the island is the Dutch word for rat's nest.

One look at the quokka's small ears, short feet (for a kangaroo), and naked tail will tell you why the early explorers mistook it for a rat. Once common in the swampy thickets of southwestern Australia, the heaviest concentration of quokkas is now on this little island, where arid conditions make existence a struggle.

Although quokkas look like rats, they are true kangaroos. There are very few of them left.

Kangaroo Island's western greys, like all kangaroos, are nocturnal. They come out of the forest to graze only when it is dark.

KANGAROO ISLAND The *western grey kangaroos* here are sooty brown instead of gray and are heavier than other members of their species. They form small mobs in the dense bushland and come into the open only to feed.

Tammar wallabies, specialized for life in dry areas, can survive a drought by drinking seawater, something no other kangaroo can do. When disturbed, the tammars sound a warning to others by thumping the ground with their hind feet. Then they make a nearly silent getaway through a maze of tunnels in the bushes.

Maybe "I don't understand you" wasn't such a funny name to give kangaroos. Two hundred years later, people still don't understand many things about them. Many marsupial mysteries wait for young scientists like you to solve them.

Bigfoot

Scientists have given the kangaroo a much more sensible name than the explorers did. They call it macropod, which means "big foot."

Their feet make kangaroos great athletes. Designed for jumping and bounding, Australia's bigfeet can clear a 10-foot fence from a standstill. Give big 'roos a running start and they can leap the length of a large school bus (about 45 feet). There isn't an animal in the world that can outjump large kangaroos and very few can outrun them. Their 40-mile-an-hour sprint-hop is faster than a race horse can run. It's not fast enough to set any records, but kangaroos don't need to. They are faster than any of the predators in Australia.

Other than humans, the dingo is the only real threat to large kangaroos. By hunting in a pack, these wild dogs can sometimes catch a kangaroo. But, as many dingoes have discovered, a bouncing kangaroo is not easy to catch. The ricochet, its two-footed hop, allows the 'roo to change direction unpredictably. By relaxing one leg and stiffening the other, it can change course in midair, going off sideways with a suddenness that four-legged runners can't match.

Most kangaroos live in grasslands dotted with rocks and bushes. The ricochet is especially suited to this type of land. Hoppers, unlike runners, don't need to detour around every little obstacle. Bounding takes them up and over.

A mob of eastern greys

Western greys ricocheting. At full speed, only their toes touch the ground.

Mammals that walk on two legs are not common. Ones that hop on two legs are even rarer. And only one hopping mammal is large—the kangaroo. All the others are small rodents: kangaroo rats, springhares, and jerboas. Like most kangaroos, the leaping rodents live in dry grasslands. It is very curious that all hopping mammals should be found in places that lack water. It's also a mystery that there aren't more mammals that hop. The ricochet gives hoppers the same rapid acceleration that cheetahs and other speed sprinters have; in addition, they don't "burn out" after a few hundred yards. Kangaroos can travel long distances because hopping uses a lot less energy than running or galloping.

The secret of the ricochet is recycled energy. It works much like a bouncing ball. A ball bounces many times without a fresh input of energy because every time it hits the ground, some of the energy is transferred to the rubber, stored there, and recycled in an elastic bounce. Kangaroos store energy in tendons, the limbs' natural elastic structures. Other animals, including humans, have tendons, which connect muscles to bone; but they aren't nearly as big as the tendons in a kangaroo's enormous feet and legs. When you run, you can store and reuse about 20 percent of your energy. Jumping kangaroos can store 70 percent of their energy and recycle it to the next leap.

Dr. Richard Taylor of Harvard University studies kangaroos' hops by putting them on a treadmill. He has discovered that when 'roos hop at full speed they do not use any more energy than they do at slower speeds. His careful measurements show that kangaroos actually use *less* energy hopping at the greater speeds. Compared with a standing animal, a ricocheting kangaroo doesn't use as much energy to breathe. Instead of using mus-cle power, which requires energy, the impact of each landing presses the air out of their lungs.

No matter how fast Dr. Taylor ran the treadmill, he found that kangaroos maintained a constant number of hops per minute. When the speed of the treadmill was increased, the kangaroos didn't hop more often; they just took bigger "steps."

Kangaroos in motion are incredibly graceful. At full speed, hopping kangaroos are completely off the ground 80 percent of the time. Their long hind legs fold and unfold, but their bodies don't bob up and down; instead, they always remain at about the same height.

One of the main reasons a kangaroo is such a good athlete is muscle power. Half its body weight is muscle. That's almost twice as much as in other animals of the same size. A kangaroo is also able to multiply that advantage. Standing naturally, a kangaroo's ankle, knee, and hip joints are bent. In a jump, they straighten like a series of extending levers and increase the power of the muscles.

At this point you might think the ricochet is the perfect way to move. It's not. Ricocheting doesn't work very well at slow speeds. To put it simply—kangaroos can't walk! The hind legs move together. Only tree kangaroos move their hind legs independently when they walk. For some reason no one understands very well, all kangaroos are able to move their back legs independently when they swim.

Punting, the kangaroo equivalent of a walk, is clumsy. To punt, a 'roo places its forefeet flat on the ground and draws its tail close behind them. With all its weight on the forefeet and tail, it swings its huge

A young western grey punting

hind legs forward and stands up. When it wants to move a short distance—while it is grazing, for instance—a kangaroo punts. The punt turns into a ricochet as the 'roo speeds up. It stands more erect, and the forelegs don't touch the ground.

Except for being webbed, a kangaroo's five-toed front paws are rather ordinary. Its long, narrow hind feet have four toes and are definitely not ordinary. The largest and strongest toe has a sharp, triangular nail. On the outside of the foot is a similar, slightly smaller toe. The toes on the inward side of the foot are connected and appear to be a single toe with a split nail. This tiny, twin toe is used mostly as a fur comb and scratching tool. The kangaroo has such fine control with this toe that it can use the nails like a pair of tweezers to pick a seed from the corner of its eye.

Groups of kangaroos are called mobs, and for good reason. Kangaroo society is totally disorganized. At the first sign of danger, 'roos bound off in all directions without leadership from the older animals. Some herd-forming animals use a

Normally very quiet, red-necked wallaby bucks grunt and click when they fight.

group defense, but kangaroos are not team players. Panic spreads quickly in a frightened mob, and the terror-stricken animals sometimes race directly *toward* the source of danger.

Rather than run, males often choose to stand and fight. They punch and scratch with their forepaws, but a serious fight always involves kicking. The hind feet are lethal weapons. Boomers are confident in their ability to defend themselves, striking out with both back feet in a monster-sized karate kick. One blow from the steel-hard claws can rip open an enemy's stomach.

A kangaroo's fancy footwork—the cliff jumping, fence leaping, and killer karate kicks—is even more impressive when you realize that it is done in the dark! All of the kangaroos are nocturnal and most of their activities take place between dusk and dawn. "Look before you leap" doesn't help kangaroos much.

Baby Factories 3

A female kangaroo is *always* pregnant. From sexual maturity (at one to two years of age) to death, a doe is seldom without three different babies: an embryo in her womb, a joey in her pouch, and a yearling by her side.

All kangaroos, like the majority of Australian mammals, are marsupials. Marsupials give birth to immature young that usually finish developing in a pouch.

Kangaroos have unusual reproduction systems—even for marsupials. Two wombs and a pouch are standard equipment for does. They are like baby factories, producing a new kangaroo every few months on an amazing assembly line of life. Some species even have a production control mechanism called diapause that halts the development of the embryo in the womb and holds it in suspended animation—an insurance policy in case the first joey dies.

Although marsupials get their name from the Latin word *marsupium*, which means "pouch," it is not their exclusive invention. Many nonmammals (frogs, seahorses, and penguins, for instance) also have pouches that provide warmth or protection. Marsupial pouches have an advantage over the others because they are the only ones that come equipped with food, in the form of milk.

Kangaroo infants are the most helpless

Tasmanian pademelon doe and joey

of all mammal babies. Their gestation period, the time spent inside the mother's womb, is extremely short. In kangaroos it is only about a month. Grey and red kangaroos, around the size of a human, give birth to young that are only three-quarters of an inch long at birth. Those of other species are no larger than a grain of rice.

Not only are the babies tiny, they are only partially formed. The newborn embryo, called a joey, has no bones, only soft cartilage. It's naked, blind, and deaf. Yet it must make its way from the birth canal to the pouch without any help.

If all goes well, the six-inch journey takes less than ten minutes. The climb is a race for life—the tiny speck can survive only a few minutes unless it reaches the pouch and immediately attaches itself to one of the four nipples inside.

A joey has strong facial muscles and begins to suck immediately. Its mouth swells around the nipple and the tiny joey

Joeys, like this yearling Bennett's wallaby, are very curious. They spend many hours exploring.

doesn't let go for many months. So that the joey doesn't bounce out, the doe keeps her pouch tightly closed. The opening is controlled by a ring of strong muscles similar to human lips. These muscles are so strong that the pouch stays waterproof even if the doe goes swimming.

When the joey is between three and eight months old, it looks like a miniature adult and begins to examine the world outside the pouch. The adventurous joey soon makes short trips outside, but it returns to nurse and sleep in the pouch. Before the joey's first birthday, the doe forces it out. Forever. This is usually to make room for a new baby. The yearling is sometimes called a joey-at-heel because it stays so close to its mother's big feet.

Kangaroos can make more babies that live to maturity than most nonmarsupial mammals can. Marsupials are not inferior, as people used to think they were. They are just different. In fact, some scientists think that the marsupial way of reproducing may be a superior adaptation to the climate of Australia.

This Bennett's wallaby doe allows her yearling to nurse even though she has a baby in the pouch.

Food 4 Stuff

Life for kangaroos is a grind. Every day, it's grind, grind, grind. Almost all of a 'roo's waking hours are spent grinding food. It has no choice. Its diet of green plants is so low in calories that it must eat *huge* quantities just to stay alive.

Don't be fooled by the kangaroo's pear-shaped body. It only *looks* fat. Even a starving kangaroo has a round belly, because it's just a holding tank for the large amount of food that must be processed every day. The only way to tell if a bigfoot has been getting enough to eat is to check the base of its tail. If you can see bones under the skin, the animal hasn't been stuffing in enough food.

One of the ways scientists classify animals is by diet. All kangaroos are herbivores, as the plant eaters are called. Because rat kangaroos don't eat green plants, they are not considered part of the kangaroo family. The large kangaroos, wallaroos, and the bigger wallabies—in fact, the overwhelming majority of true kangaroos—are grazing herbivores. Grazers eat mainly grass.

Red-necked pademelon

27

The forest-dwelling part of the family —the tree kangaroos, small wallabies, and pademelons—are browsing herbivores. Their diet is more varied. Food stuff for them may include fruit, bark, or the leaves of trees and shrubs.

Kangaroos must, obviously, kill plants in order to live. But if you think plants are helpless victims, think again. They protect themselves with poisons, nasty-tasting substances, and other chemical "weapons." Kangaroos and the other herbivores have counterweapons. Swamp wallabies, for instance, manufacture chemicals in their livers that neutralize deadly plant poisons.

Like most small kangaroos, quokkas eat both leaves and grass.

Another defense of plants is an abrasive material called silica, which wears away even the hardest teeth. Some of the grasses and ferns that kangaroos live on contain so much silica that eating them is like eating a sandpaper salad. Kangaroos can eat these silica-laden plants because they have renewable teeth. Most herbivores have grinding teeth that continue to grow throughout their lives. But kangaroos, elephants, and some other plant eaters adopted a different system: moving molars. Their chewing teeth, which form at the back of the jaw, slowly move forward. When a worn-out molar reaches the front of the row, it falls out. That may sound like a perfect system, but there's a catch. Kangaroos can only produce about sixteen molars. If a kangaroo lives an especially long time (twenty years), all the teeth get used up. Toothless kangaroos cannot chew food properly and starve to death.

Most mammals have two bones in their lower jaw that are joined together and act as one. But kangaroos' lower jaw bones are joined by a flexible ligament and can move separately. The purpose of this unusual connection remained a mystery until a slow-motion X-ray film of a feeding red-necked wallaby revealed the secret. The lower jaw moves downward, forward, and *apart* when the animal reaches for grass or leaves. The widespread lower jaw lets a kangaroo grab more food, which it rips away with an upward jerk of the head. The food moves across an empty space where the tongue arranges the pieces into wads and passes them to the grinding molars, which crush the vegetation with rapid side-to-side movements.

The grazing species bend forward and put their forefeet flat on the ground when they eat. Swinging their heads, they snip all the grass within reach, first on one side and then the other. A path of closely cropped grass about a yard wide reveals where the four-legged lawnmower has fed. Browsers eat sitting up, holding leaves or branches in their small forepaws.

Watching kangaroos eat is usually about

as exciting as watching grass grow. Macropods are very businesslike about eating and don't do anything else for hours. This is frustrating to kangaroo watchers, who are always hoping to see something unusual like the time when, just after dawn, a doe in a mob of Bennett's wallabies caught our attention. She was acting very peculiarly, throwing back her head and making terrible choking noises. The choking turned into a coughing fit and green juice dribbled from the corners of her mouth. Finally, with an enormous gag, she vomited a wad of partially digested grass into her mouth. Obviously contented at last, the doe settled down and chewed the

A mob scene. All large kangaroos and most of the large wallabies, such as these Bennetts, graze in groups.

mess. Believe it or not, we were delighted. After months of waiting, we had finally seen a kangaroo chew its cud.

Ruminant herbivores have multiple stomachs and chew their food twice. The partially digested grass of the second chewing is called a cud. Their saliva contains chemicals that help process the food. Kangaroos have super-smelly spit—so stinky that sheep often refuse to eat where kangaroos have drooled on the grass.

Mammals can't digest cellulose, the stiffener found in most green plants. How then are herbivores able to survive? With the aid of specialized bacteria, that's how. Billions of cellulose-digesting bacteria live in a kangaroo's stomach. The 'roo isn't in danger. In fact, it couldn't live without them. They and the 'roo are biological buddies: two completely different organisms that live together in a relationship that benefits both of them. This relationship is called symbiosis. In this case, the bacteria get a nice place to grow and multiply. The kangaroo provides their food: lots of green plants and a nitrogen-rich

Red-legged pademelons must keep a lookout for danger while they eat.

substance that its body manufactures from waste products.

The kangaroo benefits because the bacteria turn the plants' indigestible cellulose into usable sugars and starches. They make enough for themselves *and* the kangaroo. It's not a complete diet, though; some essential fats and proteins are missing. However, through a sneaky and rather dirty trick, the kangaroo gets those nutrients from its "buddies" by eating a few billion of the bacteria every day.

The Survival Experts

Compared to kangaroos, camels are amateurs at desert survival. No water leaves a kangaroo's body unless it is absolutely necessary. Droppings are as dry as hay, and some species have such concentrated urine that it solidifies when it is exposed to air. Rock wallabies that live in desert areas are so adapted to dry conditions that even when water is available, they don't drink. Never. Not ever. Not even when the temperature is 120 degrees Fahrenheit.

How do kangaroos survive without water? They don't. A few species survive without *drinking,* but not without water.

Australia is now the driest habitable continent, but millions of years ago it was cooler and wetter. Plants and animals that couldn't adjust to the changes became extinct. Most of Australia became hot and dry, and the majority of kangaroos adapted to cope with those conditions. Small species learned to live on the water in the plants they ate and became experts at conserving moisture. Large ones developed the ability to survive journeys across territories of three hundred square miles in search of fresh grass and water. Not all kangaroos can withstand long periods without water, though. It takes millions of generations to become adapted. Without water, rain-forest kangaroos, for instance, would die from dehydration in a very short time.

Desert plants are also experts at surviv-

Tammar wallaby

33

ing in dry places. They protect their water supply by storing it underground during the day, releasing it to nourish the leaves only at night. So kangaroos became moonlight munchers, eating when the leaves have the maximum amount of water. All kangaroos and 90 percent of Australia's other marsupials are nocturnal, resting and conserving water by day and eating by night.

Greys and the smaller forest-dwelling kangaroos pass the daylight hours snoozing in the deepest shade of the woods. Rock wallabies seek out cool, dark caves to keep from overheating. The nailtail 'roos find hollow logs to hide in, and hare wallabies nap under bushes just as rabbits do. If kangaroos of the open grasslands can't find shade, they dig shallow holes, which protect them from reflected heat.

Australian summers are so hot that kangaroos can overheat even in the shade. But keeping cool is "no sweat." Literally. Kangaroos *can't* sweat because they have no sweat glands. Instead, they lick gobs of sticky, bubbly saliva onto their arms and paws. The skin there is almost bare of fur, and the evaporating spit cools the blood as it runs through veins close to the surface.

Licking isn't a very practical method of heat control. In an emergency, it's not very convenient to stop and lick your arms. Kangaroos have an alternate way to

An overheated eastern grey 'roo cools off.

cool off—panting. It's usually saved for panic situations, because panting, like licking, uses a lot of water.

Kangaroos can regulate the *amount* of heat sent to various parts of the body. At night, when they are most active, only the central core of the body stays warm. The temperature of the legs is lowered to conserve energy. Some desert people, including Australian aborigines (who live in the same places as kangaroos do), also have the ability to control heat flow in this way.

Birth control is important to animals that live in places without a predictable pattern of rainfall. If kangaroos were born during droughts, they would die. But they aren't. The 'roos' reproductive system needs chemicals found in green plants. When they can't find food, they can't give birth. In some species, diapause delays birth till the time is favorable. These methods of birth control are very effective in maintaining a healthy balance between the number of kangaroos and the ability of the land to support them.

Bennetts' long fur is an adaptation to cold climates.

Australia is a continent with many environments, and the members of the macropod family have adapted to all of them.

Tree kangaroos had to make dietary adaptations so they could survive on leaves, the primary food source in their rain-forest home. Leaves have more toxins, or poisons, than grasses do. So tree kangaroos learned to get by with fewer of the poison-packed leaves. The price of this efficient system is less energy. That's why kangaroo watchers say the favorite activity of tree kangaroos is *no* activity. Tree kangaroos had to make body adjustments, too. Although ancestral 'roos were tree dwellers, today's tree kangaroos did not descend directly from them but from tree dwellers that had adapted to ground living. To live in the trees again, their feet became shorter and more flexible; forelimbs grew longer and stronger; and big claws evolved to help them climb.

Cliff-dwelling kangaroos underwent body changes to help them survive in a rocky existence. Their leg muscles became bigger and stronger and that made jumping uphill easier. Their feet became more thickly padded to cushion the shock of landing on rocks, and knobby soles, sort of a marsupial version of sneakers, developed to give better traction.

Bigfeet live in snowy mountains and steamy swamps, in rain forests and deserts, in woodlands and on the open plains. In terms of numbers, kangaroos are the

Western greys lie in shallow holes during the day.

most successful mammal in Australia. Their story is one of animals in tune with the land, survival experts with 25 million years of experience.

Is the kangaroo in danger? The answer is yes and no.

Millions of kangaroos still roam the Land Down Under. There are, in fact, more kangaroos today than at any other

They throw dirt over themselves to keep insects away.

garoos have often benefited. The clearing of forests and planting of grass for cattle and sheep has been good for the grass-eating kangaroos, too. Wells drilled for domestic stock have opened up vast areas where kangaroos never had dependable water before.

On the other hand, the number of small kangaroos has declined over the past two hundred years. Imported grazers such as rabbits have cut their food supply. And they are defenseless against cats, foxes, and other imported predators. Some of the small kangaroos are now extinct on the mainland and exist only in tiny populations on small protected offshore islands that are kept free of predators.

Australians have done well in protecting their native wildlife. Only six species of kangaroos have disappeared. Kangaroos *can* change to fit the new face of the land, but they need time. Evolution takes lots of time. That is why we must do everything we can to protect kangaroos now so that they will be able to hop into the future.

time in history. More than there were when the aborigines arrived and *many* more than there were two hundred years ago when the Europeans first landed. Today, kangaroos outnumber humans in Australia ten to one.

Not all of the changes that humans have brought about in Australia's environment have been bad for kangaroos. Large kan-

Kangaroo Facts

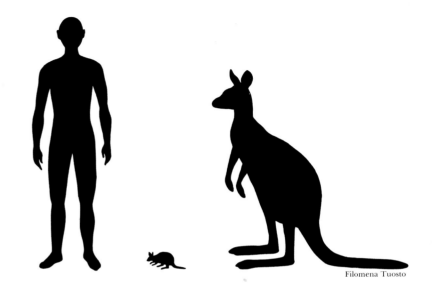

Filomena Tuosto

Common Names: Kangaroo, wallaby, euro, forester, wallaroo, pademelon
Male: buck, boomer *Female:* doe, flier *Baby:* joey
Group: mob

Scientific Names: Macropodidae (family). There are 60 species in 8 genera.

Size: Males are larger than females in all species. Smallest: female warabi rock wallaby (2 pounds); largest: male red and grey kangaroos (200 pounds).

Speed: 40 mph in sprint (1 or 2 miles); 20 mph for long distances (10 miles or more).

Color: Solid gray, brown, black, yellow, red, tan, blue, or patterned. Brindle, stripes, and decorations are common. Occasionally albino (solid white).

Behavior: Nocturnal. Some species also active at dawn and dusk. Shy.

Habitat/Range: Australia and nearby islands of Tasmania and New Guinea. All ecosystems from swamp and rain forest to mountains and desert.

Food: Vegetation, including grass, leaves, fruits, seeds, and roots.

Life Span: Twenty years in captivity; approximately six in wild.

Gestation: One young after gestation ranging from 28 to 36 days depending on species.

Native predators: All species: humans and dingoes; small species: Tasmanian devils; young of small species: eagles, goanna lizards, pythons.

Population: Estimated at 100 million. Some species common; others endangered.

Index